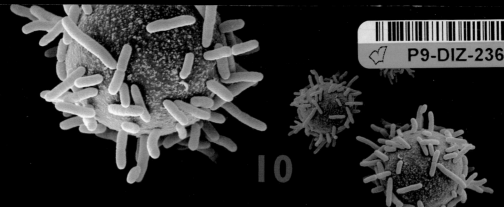

Features

Wigging Out

Hundreds of years ago, people thought it was stylish to have really big hair. Rich people often had the biggest hair because they could buy large, fancy wigs. Those people were called "big wigs." Today, you don't need huge hair to be called a bigwig. You just have to be important.

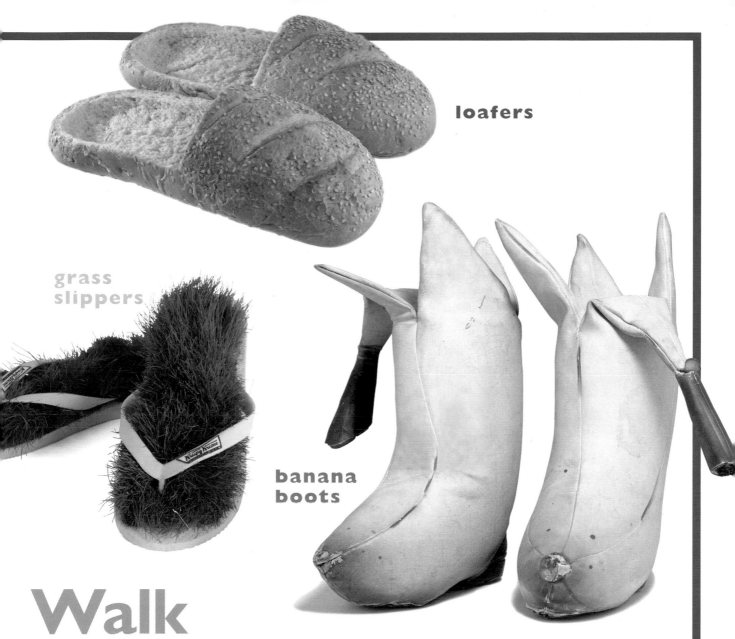

loafers

grass slippers

banana boots

Walk on the Wild Side

How would you like a pair of banana boots? Or would you rather loaf in a pair of loafers? If you like to walk barefoot in the grass, you might want sandals with real grass growing from the soles. When it comes to funny footwear, there is no limit to what you can do. What kind of shoes would you wear if you let your feet and your imagination run wild?

Funny Egg-speriment

You can make eggs that will bounce! If you don't believe it, follow the steps below and see for yourself.

1. **Place a hard-boiled egg in a glass.**
2. **Cover the egg with vinegar.**
3. **Let the egg soak for 3 days.**
4. **Take the egg out and gently rinse it with water.**
5. **Drop the egg on the sidewalk.**

How does it work? Eggshells are full of calcium (say it: CAL-see-um). Calcium is what makes the shells so hard. Vinegar makes calcium get soft. If you soak a hard-boiled egg in vinegar long enough, the shell will get so soft it won't break. The egg will bounce! Now that's wild!

Funky Chickens

There are hundreds of different kinds of chickens in the world. Some of them, like this crested chicken, look pretty funky. You don't see wild-looking chickens very often because most farmers don't raise them. Farmers want chickens that lay lots of eggs, and most fancy chickens don't lay many eggs. They sure are fun to look at, though!

A Wild Word

"Wild" may be a small word, but it can be used in lots of ways. How many different meanings for **"wild"** can you find in this issue? Here are some to get you started!

Untamed:
Jane studied wild animals in Africa.

Fantastic:
Mike has a **wild** imagination!

Out of control:
People get sick when germs run **wild** in their bodies.

Extremely stormy:
Those dark clouds mean we're in for some **wild** weather.

Extremely enthusiastic:
Elena's **wild** about cats. She's read seven books about them!

Zap!

There's no weather that's flashier than a lightning storm. Lightning bolts are made of electricity. The electricity builds up in the air during stormy weather. Lightning bolts can jump from cloud to cloud, making wild loops and patterns as they go. There have even been lightning bolts over 75 miles long! ★

Friends in the Wild

Young Jane when she first
began studying chimps

Jane Goodall stepped outside of her tent deep in the African jungle. She heard a rustling in the brush. A tiny chimpanzee crawled into view. It was Flint, a baby chimp she had been studying. Jane crouched down and reached out her hand. Slowly, Flint reached out his little hand to meet hers. Jane smiled. She loved her job!

Jane was one of the first scientists to live with chimps in the wild. Other scientists studied chimps in zoos. Jane studied them in the wild because she wanted to learn how they lived and behaved in their natural home. Over time, the chimps learned that Jane was their friend. She was able to get close enough to see things no other scientists had seen.

Jane spent more than 25 years studying chimps in the wild. Because of her work, we know important things about chimps. Turn the page to meet some of the chimps she studied.

Jane lived in a tent in the jungle. Only a few helpers and her family lived there with her. There were many dangers in the wild. Baboons stole food from the camp. Dangerous buffalo and leopards (say it: LEPP-urds) lived nearby. Poisonous insects and snakes came into her tent when it rained! But Jane thought it was all worth it to be near the chimps.

Scientists used to think that only humans could make and use tools. Jane proved that's not true. Chimps make their own tools too! In fact, chimps use more objects as tools than any other animal except for humans. A male chimp named Gremlin used a twig as a tool to get food. He peeled the leaves off of the twig and stuck it into a mound of dirt where termites lived. Then he ate the termites, using the twig as a spoon.

Jane learned that chimps help each other. She observed a chimp named Melissa helping her friend, Gimble, by picking bugs out of her fur. Chimps also show friendship by hugging, kissing, and sharing food.

Jane had been studying chimps for many years when this picture was taken.

Jane saw that chimps sometimes fought with each other over who should be the leader of the group. She also noticed that chimps had many ways to offer comfort to one another. After a chimp named Goblin got into a fight with the other chimps, his friend Frodo patted him on the back.

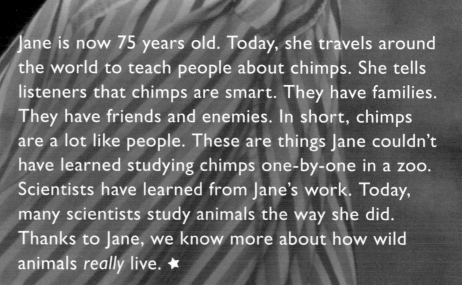

Jane is now 75 years old. Today, she travels around the world to teach people about chimps. She tells listeners that chimps are smart. They have families. They have friends and enemies. In short, chimps are a lot like people. These are things Jane couldn't have learned studying chimps one-by-one in a zoo. Scientists have learned from Jane's work. Today, many scientists study animals the way she did. Thanks to Jane, we know more about how wild animals *really* live. ★

Ewww! Germs!

Achoo! You've probably had a nasty cold or flu at some time. And you probably know it was caused by germs. But hundreds of years ago, people had some wild ideas about why they got sick. Some people believed evil spirits caused sickness. Others believed that bad smells could make them ill.

Then, along came a man named Antoni van Leeuwenhoek [say it: LAY-ven-hook]. In his spare time, he made a microscope and used it to look at things around him. Through the microscope, he saw extremely tiny living things. They were things no one had ever seen before.

Microscope

Antoni didn't know it, but he had discovered germs. Germs are too small to see without a microscope. In fact, germs are so small that thousands of them could fit in the period at the end of this sentence. Even though scientists everywhere began studying these tiny beings, it took hundreds of years before people understood that germs caused sickness.

Today, we know that some germs help your body stay healthy and other germs can make you sick. These pictures of germs were taken using a powerful microscope. Up close, the germs look cool but the sickness they cause is definitely *not* cool!

These tiny red germs can poison your blood.

The yellow spots are cold germs!

These multi-colored germs can cause the flu.

If these little white germs get in your food, they can make you very sick.

11

Luckily, our bodies have many tricks for stopping germs before they run wild and make us sick. Your nose is lined with tiny hairs. When you breathe, the hairs catch germs in the air before they move further into your body. A sneeze sends the germs back out where they came from. Your tears help wash away germs that enter your eyes. Here are some other ways your body battles germs:

Your skin acts like armor. Germs can get past your skin and into your body only when your skin is broken by a cut or scratch.

Your stomach produces a strong acid that can kill some of the germs that may be in food you eat.

If germs do get into your body, your body can still fight them. Your blood contains special white cells that kill germs by eating them!

How Germs Get Around

This experiment will help you see one way germs spread — and a great way to stop them!

Sprinkle a bit of glitter into your right hand. Pretend each flake of glitter is a "germ." Rub your hands together. Now, shake hands with a few friends. Ask these friends to shake hands with a few other friends.

Now, ask everyone to look at their hands. Did the "glitter germs" spread? How can you stop them?

Wash your hands with soap and water, of course! How long do you need to wash before all the glitter is gone? ★

You will need:

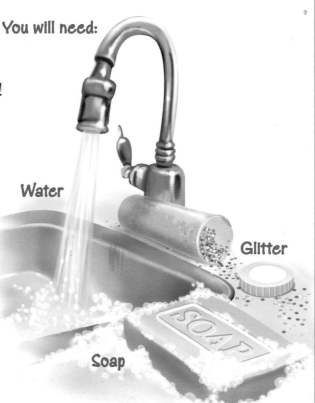

Water

Glitter

Soap

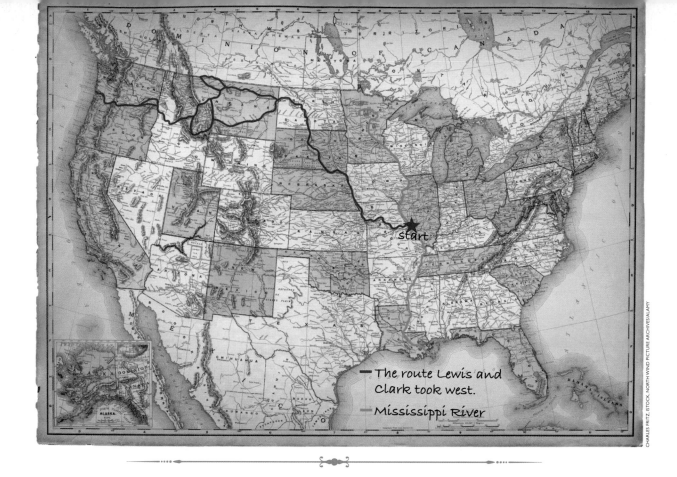

start

The route Lewis and Clark took west.

Mississippi River

Exploring the Wild

America is a vast land with oceans on either side and a wide river, called the Mississippi, running down the middle. Today we can go from ocean to ocean by car, train, or plane. But 200 years ago, no one knew what the land west of the Mississippi was like. President Thomas Jefferson wanted to know. He sent a band of explorers to find out.

Jefferson chose a young man named Meriwether Lewis to lead the explorers. Lewis and his friend, William Clark, were smart, brave, and eager for adventure. They began their journey in 1804, joined by a crew of about 40 men. The crew set out on boats on the Missouri River, just west of the Mississippi. They would follow the river as far as it would take them. Then they hoped to continue west until they reached the Pacific Ocean.

May 14, 1804

I set out at 4 p.m. under a gentle breeze up the Missouri.

There were no cameras and no phones when Lewis and Clark made their trek. Instead, they kept careful notes in journals. They drew pictures of the unusual animals and plants they saw. Thanks to these journals, we can hear in their own words about all the exciting things that happened along the way.

15

December 7, 1804

Captain Lewis took
15 men and joined the
Indians on horseback,
who were killing buffalo.
Three men got frostbit
very badly.

The journey wasn't easy. During their first winter, the temperature dipped to 40 degrees below zero. Many members of the crew fell ill with flu and other sicknesses. Food was scarce.

The land they passed through seemed wild and dangerous to Lewis and Clark, but it was already home to the American Indians they met along the way. Many Indians gave food to Lewis and Clark's crew and helped them hunt. An American Indian woman named Sacagawea (say it: sah-cah-ga-WAY-a) served as a very important guide along their journey.

"IN AN INSTANT THE MONSTER RAN AT US..." CHARLES FRITZ

During the second year of the journey, the crew faced more hardships. One evening, they met up with a large grizzly bear. Four of the men shot the bear, but still it charged at them. The bear came so close that the men dropped their guns and jumped into the river. Finally, one of the men who stayed on shore shot the bear through the head and killed him.

The worst was still to come when the crew made their way through the snowy, rugged Bitterroot mountains. It was so hard to find food

May 14, 1805

In an instant this monster ran at them with open mouth.

September 3, 1805

We passed over some of the worst road that horses ever passed. Our horses frequently fell.

"CROSSING THE MOST TERRIBLE MOUNTAINS WE EVER BEHELD" CHARLES FRITZ

that the crew had to kill and eat their horses. They even ate candles and bear grease. In the bitter cold, many crew members got frostbite. Clark was afraid they would starve or freeze to death. Luckily, he found an American Indian nation at the foot of the mountains. The Nez Perce people, as they were called, gave the starving explorers food and shelter.

October 15, 1805

This river is very handsome, except at the rapids, where it is risking both life and property to pass.

The Nez Perce people also taught Lewis and Clark's crew to make canoes by digging out the centers of large logs. Using the dugout canoes, the crew hoped to follow the Columbia River all the way to the Pacific Ocean. But the river was swift and treacherous. The swirling water overturned one canoe. Another canoe was split open on the rocks. The crew didn't give up. They kept paddling until they got to the end of the river, where it met the rolling, blue waters of the Pacific Ocean. "Our goal is reached at last!" wrote Clark in his journal.

The crew returned east with many exciting tales to tell. Their dangerous journey had taken nearly two years. (Today, you can drive the same route in six days.) Along the way, they had discovered 178 new plants and 122 new animals that before only Indians had known about. They made peaceful contact with nearly 50 American Indian nations. Above all, they showed a way through the wilderness for others to follow. America could be settled from ocean to ocean and become the nation we know today. ★

November 7, 1805

Ocean in view! O, the joy!

THE PACIFIC FROM POINT OF CLARK'S VIEW, JANUARY 8, 1806. CHARLES FRITZ

A *WILD* Imagination

The man standing in this strange land seems confused. It's no wonder. The reflections of the swans in the lake look like elephants! Where is this place? Is it real? How did he get there?

He got there in the dreams of Salvador Dali (say it: DAH-lee), a famous artist with a wild imagination. Dali started painting about a hundred years ago. Back then, most people thought that an artist should draw or paint pictures of things exactly as they were. Dali didn't think so. He made art that looked like his dreams. Dreams don't always make sense, so Dali's art looked unreal, or *surreal* (say it: suh-REEL). A lot of people didn't like it. Take a look at some of Dali's work and see what *you* think.

Dali was not the only artist to make art about his dreams. Other artists did it too, but Dali got more attention than they did because Dali did so many other crazy things. Once Dali rode in a fancy car full of cauliflower. Another time, he gave a speech in a diving suit. People were always wondering what Dali would do next!

It wasn't long before people all over the world knew of Salvador Dali and his strange art. After a while, people got used to Dali's wild style. Because of Dali and other artists like him, people learned that paintings don't have to look realistic to be good. Today they go to museums to see them!

This is Dali's most famous painting. Do you think the idea for this painting came from a dream?

Can you see a woman's face in this painting? It's a picture of Dali's wife.

Wacky Whiskers

Dali made all kinds of art, not just paintings. Dali and a friend liked to take photos. They made an entire book just about Dali's mustache! Did you ever think a mustache could be worn in so many silly ways? Did you ever think a mustache could be art? ★

Survive in the Wild

Good advice we hope you'll never need!

How to Deal with an Angry Gorilla

Gorillas are usually peaceful, unless they think you're trying to be the boss. A gorilla may pretend to come after you, just to show you who's in charge. What should you do? Don't look at his face. Stay quiet and keep your arms by your sides. If he thinks you get his point, he won't start a fight with you.

How to Get Along with Tarantulas

A tarantula is a furry spider about the size of a tennis ball. It may be big and hairy, but it's not that dangerous. If it bites you, it usually causes nothing more than swelling. Still, who wants to get that far? If a tarantula visits you, find a stick and gently poke it. The tarantula will probably wander off. If it crawls onto you, start bouncing up and down. Shake that spider off!

How to Escape a Python's Hug

The python is the world's longest snake. This giant snake kills its prey by squeezing it. How do you escape the Hug of Doom? Relax your muscles. This may trick the snake into thinking you're already dead. He may loosen his grip. If so, grab his head and start unwrapping the snake from your body.

How to Survive a Charging Rhinoceros

If a rhinoceros (say it: rye-NOSS-er-us) lowers its head and snorts at you, it's got one thing on its mind. It wants to stab you with its horn. You can't outrun a rhino. Instead, look for a tree and climb it. No tree? Get as far into thick bushes as you can. Once the rhino has run past you, run the other way. It's hard for a rhino to turn around. Once they get going in one direction, they're not likely to come back. ★

What's so grand about the Grand Canyon?

The Grand Canyon is a vast hole in the earth in the state of Arizona. If you've ever stood on the edge of it, you know that it's a magical sight. Look out, and the canyon seems to stretch out forever. Look down, and you may feel dizzy. The bottom of the canyon is more than a mile beneath your feet!

The Grand Canyon began forming millions of years ago. Deep underground, two pieces of the earth bumped up against each other. The land was forced up into the sky. This created a plateau (say it: pla-TOH), or a mountain that's flat on top. The Colorado River flowed over the plateau. Water is very powerful when it flows through an area for many years. Rivers can make big changes by washing away small amounts of rock at a time. Over millions of years, the river carved deep gashes in the plateau. The result was the huge, beautiful Grand Canyon.

What if the Grand Canyon's beauty had been ruined? What if people had bought the land and built homes, highways, mines, and factories on it? Luckily, that didn't happen, and it never will. The Grand Canyon is one of 58 national parks that have been saved as wilderness. National parks preserve what's wild and wonderful about our country. We can enjoy them, learn from them, and take in their beauty. Isn't that grand? ★

Wild About BOOKS

What is your favorite book, and why do you like it?

Sonic the Hedgehog. I like Sonic because he runs fast. He **fights crazy bad guys** and he always wins.

Tyler, age 7

The Skin I'm In. It's a fun book. I learned that it **doesn't matter what color skin you have.**

Kennedy, age 8

The *Rainbow Magic* books. Each one is about a different fairy. They're a **little bit frightening but fun.**

Anna, age 8

Cats: Little Tigers in Your House. I have a cat and a dog, and I want to **learn more** about how they act.

Elena, age 8

Captain Underpants. The **characters act silly.**

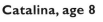

Catalina, age 8

Flat Stanley. It **makes me laugh!**

Joe, age 7

Magic Tree House series. I like to read adventurous books because you kind of get scared at times but you know it **ends well.**

Rebecca, age 7

Be a Bookworm

Try these great books:

Dear Max
Max writes letters to his favorite author who, much to his surprise, writes back.

How Many Ways Can You Catch a Fly?
This amazing science book is full of facts about how animals escape danger.

Ivy and Bean Break the Fossil Record
Two buddies dig for dinosaur bones in the backyard.

Planting the Trees of Kenya
Meet an inspiring woman who helped change the world.

Stink: The Incredible Shrinking Kid
In this funny story, one boy believes he is shrinking. ★

Go Bananas

You'll go wild for this dessert!

You will need:

A banana, peeled and sliced

2 plates

Wax paper

Toothpicks

A bowl

Magic Shell™ topping

Confetti sprinkles

1 PUT banana slices on a plate with wax paper. Stick a toothpick in the center of each slice. Put the plate in the freezer. When frozen, take the slices out of the freezer.

2 SQUEEZE topping into the bowl. Hold a banana slice by the toothpick. Dip the slice into the topping until it's covered.

3 BEFORE the topping hardens, hold the slice over the other plate and drop sprinkles onto the banana. Set the slice back on the wax paper.

4 REPEAT

the steps with
the other slices.
Wait for the
topping to
harden and
serve frozen! ★

THE AUTHOR FROM THE BLACK LAGOON

Mike Thaler has written more than 32 Black Lagoon books.

Meet Mike Thaler, author of the Black Lagoon books. How did he become a writer? Where does he get his wild ideas? He'll tell you all about it!

I have always loved to create things. As a child, I loved crayons, but not coloring books. I always wanted to draw my own lines.

I had always thought I would be a teacher when I grew up until I took a test that asked,

> Would you rather:
> a. Ride a kangaroo?
> b. Sit under a flower?
> c. Write a poem?

I answered, "Write a poem," and the test results told me, "You are an artist."

TEXT ADAPTED FROM IMAGINATION BY MIKE THALER, © 2002 FROM THE MEET THE AUTHOR COLLECTION. PUBLISHED BY RICHARD C. OWEN PUBLISHERS, INC. KATONAH, NY 10536—WWW.RCOWEN.COM

So, in college, I studied art and learned to draw. Later, I studied English and learned to write. I believed I would become a famous cartoonist. Well, that never happened, but a lot else did.

One day, I got a call from a children's book editor. She had seen a cartoon I drew. She asked if I had ever thought of writing a children's book. I said, "Yes!"

That night, I wrote a book called *Magic Boy*. The next day, the editor decided to publish it. Since then I have published more than 240 children's books.

Though I drew the pictures for the first five books I wrote, I soon realized that a professional illustrator could do a much better job. In 1981, artist Jared Lee illustrated one of my books, *A Hippopotamus Ate the Teacher*. Since then, we have done lots and lots of books together.

Our best known series is "The Black Lagoon." I had the idea for the title from a movie called *Creature from the Black Lagoon*.

Kids ask me why I write the Black Lagoon books. Well, I love to laugh and to make others laugh. I love to create things. Want to see how I do it? Turn the page!

Mike Thaler

HOW TO WRITE A WILD STORY

To write a wild story, you need a starting point. You start with an idea, like a seed, that can grow and blossom.

THE IDEA

The food in the school lunchroom is ALIVE!

Okay, that's our seed. Now where are we going to take it?

Out of the pans...and across the lunchroom floor.

The food eats the lunch lady.

It eats the principal.

Okay, how can we get wilder? Where do we go from here? Keep building the story. Make each thing that happens crazier and crazier.

The kids call the sheriff. The food chases him out of the school.

The kids call the fire department. No luck.

They call the Army. No luck. They call the Air Force. No luck.

Now our story is at a turning point. At the turning point, you begin to resolve your story. You build and build, but a good story always has a satisfying ending. So who can the kids call? They can call on Mickey. Mickey will eat anything!

Mickey walks calmly to the food. He takes out two spoons.

Because we don't want anyone to really be hurt, the food burps out:

the cafeteria lady...

the principal...

the soldiers.

Now it's just the food and Mickey. It's a showdown. The food looks at Mickey. Mickey looks at the food. What will happen?

The food moves closer, and closer, and closer. Mickey's spoons flash in the sunlight and...

He eats it! He eats it all!

Wow! We all cheer.

Now it's time to wrap up your story and tie the bow.

The mayor gives Mickey a medal for saving the school.

Mickey looks at the medal. He smiles.

And he eats it!

Want to grow your own wild story?

Here are some seeds to get you started:

★ I woke up this morning and my bed was on the ceiling!

★ One day the clown's smile flew away.

★ I think I'll build Frankenstein for my science project.

★ One day, I wanted to see how far my rubber band would stretch.

Use these ideas or look into your own imagination. It is full of seeds. You just have to look for them. Then plant them in a story and let them run wild! ★

OUCH!

ABBY CARTER

Dear Ouch,

When is it okay to talk about somebody? Is it ever okay to gossip?

Wondering

Most people like to chat about people and things around them. It's one way we feel like part of the group. But sometimes the things kids say about others are hurtful. Sometimes the information is private, or it's just not true. There is an easy way to know if it's okay to talk about someone else. Just ask yourself: would I want someone to say this about me? If the answer is no, keep your lips zipped!

Dear Ouch,

I can't wait for summer. During the week I get really impatient at school. How do I stop thinking about summer and pay attention?

Can't wait

It's fun to look forward to summer. But daydreaming about it during school will only make summer seem farther away. Instead, make a list of everything you're most excited to do this summer. Put it in a special place at home. Don't look at it until the school year ends. No peeking! Once summer comes, get out the list. Have fun checking off things as you do them.

OUCH!

Dear Ouch,

My friends tease me about what I wear. Even when I'm just wearing my regular jeans they laugh at me. It makes me feel bad. How can I make them stop?

Feeling Down

Kids tease other kids to make themselves feel important. Show them that their unkind words don't bring you down. Tell your friends it doesn't matter what they think about your clothes because you're comfortable wearing them. In the meantime, get to know other kids who make you feel good no matter what outfit you're wearing. True friends don't care more about your clothes than they do about the person inside them.

Dear Ouch,

I'm having a birthday party. My mom says I can only invite six kids. But I have more friends than that! What should I do?

Birthday Girl

The key word here is kindness. Invite the friends you feel closest to. But hand out invitations away from school, or mail them to your friends' homes. And be sure you don't talk about the party in front of other kids. You can set up special playdates with friends you couldn't invite. ★

After School

Do you know what happens in the school at night
When the teachers all leave and turn out the light?

The math books count out, "3, 2, 1!"
Then the clock on the wall shouts, "Time for fun!"

The erasers start to race around the floor.
The rubber stamps stamp right out of the drawer.

The scissors cut up, and the stickers peel out.
The paper clips twist, the globe spins about.

The flag waves, "Bye-bye! Don't be late!"
As the wall calendar goes out on a date.

The telephone gives the map a ring.
The ruler gets bossy and acts like a king.

The glue sticks together and the pencils point,
Till the class bell clangs, "Clean up this joint!"

So if something in your desk doesn't look just right,
Maybe it's because of what happened last night. ★

By Carol Diggory Shields

DON'T LOOK DOWN!

Visitors to this skyscraper in Chicago can gaze down on the city from 103 stories high. This glass-bottom platform makes it feel like they're hanging in midair. It's one wild way to see the world! ★

$1.29

890526
g140-
077-0

No Exchange
Media
Books

Rowland Reading Foundation
Middleton, Wisconsin

ISBN 978-1-59833-492-0
9000

9 781598 334920

SG3

ANNE RYAN/zrHMAGES/CORBIS